Basic Prep

Helen July

ISBN 978-1-68517-873-4 (paperback)
ISBN 978-1-68517-874-1 (digital)

Copyright © 2022 by Helen July

All rights reserved. No part of this publication may be reproduced, distributed, or transmitted in any form or by any means, including photocopying, recording, or other electronic or mechanical methods without the prior written permission of the publisher. For permission requests, solicit the publisher via the address below.

Christian Faith Publishing
832 Park Avenue
Meadville, PA 16335
www.christianfaithpublishing.com

Printed in the United States of America

Contents

Questions to Ask Yourself Before You Get Started 5
Week 1 (Genesis 2:18–25): His Help 7
Week 2 (1 Corinthians 7:1–16): His Body 10
Week 3 (1 Peter 3:1–12): His Example..14
Week 4 (Ephesians 5:22–33): His Strength 18
Week 5 (1 Corinthians 13:4–8a): His Love 22
Week 6 (Galatians 5:22): His Fruit..25

Questions to Ask Yourself Before You Get Started

What is God saying about my marriage?
Am I willing to do what it takes?
Am I ready to be open and honest?
Am I ready to let God help me?
Am I willing to love my husband *unconditionally* as God loves me?
Am I ready to let the fruit of the Spirit be my response to my husband every time and all the time?

Week 1: His Help

In the beginning, when God created Eve, He created her from Adam's rib to be his help. The woman was taken from Adam's rib, which protects his heart, so I believe we are the protector of our husband's heart. But as women, we need first to understand that for our husbands to be right, we, as wives, have to be right first. Think about it this way: if you have a business and your employees or your helpers are not doing the job they were hired for, your business will not succeed. This is the same thing with marriage; if we are not doing our job as the helper of our husband in our marriage, how do we expect our marriage to be successful?

Ladies, we have to be willing to take a long hard look at ourselves and stop looking at what our husbands are doing and not doing. Instead, we have to start building our relationship with the Father, sitting at his feet and getting the instructions on how to rebuild our marriages and be the help our husbands need. Remember you are not married to your husband by mistake. If God doesn't allow it, then it can't happen.

Notes:_____
_____
_____
_____
_____
_____
_____
_____
_____

Read Genesis 2:21–25.

As you read this, ask God to help you understand what it is that He wants you to know and how to be the help that your husband needs.

Pray.

Always pray over your husband in the morning before he leaves or you leave. Pray for his protection, peace, job, joy and for his footsteps to be ordered and led by God. Pray for him before he goes to sleep at night that he will have rest and peace in his sleep so he can hear from the Lord clearly. And pray for him throughout the day, every day.

Homework

God, what are you saying to me about my marriage?

BASIC PREP

When you ask the question, you have to be ready and willing to hear GOD's response. At the beginning of our marriage, the Lord told me that He was going to use our marriage to help other marriages. I laughed at that time because I did not see how this could be. We hadn't even been married a year, so how could I tell anyone about something I knew nothing about myself. But God saw what I had not yet seen, He knew what I did not yet know, and He understood what I did not yet understand. But now I know.

Week 2: His Body

Contrary to worldly belief, the Bible says that the wife's body is not hers alone, but it belongs to her husband. The world would beg to differ by saying it's your body and no one can tell you what to do with your body. The world would say that if your husband does not do what you want him to do, you need to withhold sex from him. This is not what the word of God says; it says the exact opposite. The Bible lets us know that there is only one reason to abstain from sex in marriage, and that is if the two of you agree to do so for fasting and prayer, but then you are to return back to each other.

Ladies, we have to STOP conforming to the world's way of thinking, and let GOD transform us by having a new mind. It's time to take our marriages back by returning to God's word and allowing the Holy Spirit to lead and guide us back into His truth. The one thing I told my husband when we got married was that I would never deny him sex, and I never did. I had seen and heard women talk about how they would not have sex with their husbands unless he (fill in the blank). I never agreed with that, and I saw their marriages suffer because of this worldly way of thinking.

Notes:_____
_____
_____
_____
_____
_____
_____
_____
_____

BASIC PREP

Read 1 Corinthians 7:1–16 and Song of Songs (Song of Solomon).

As you read this, ask God to help you understand what it is that He wants you to know and how can this help you fulfill your husband's needs that are pleasing to both God and your husband.

Pray.

Cover your sex life in prayer.

Pray and ask God to help you not withhold sex from your husband and not use sex as a weapon or a tool to negotiate to get your way. Instead, ask God to teach you how to use sex the way He intended it to be between husband and wife.

BASIC PREP

Homework

The next thing we have to ask is am I willing to do what it takes?

_____
_____
_____
_____
_____
_____
_____
_____
_____
_____
_____
_____
_____
_____

When you ask the question, you have to be ready and willing to hear GOD's response. Sometimes doing what it takes isn't always easy or what we want to do. But we have to be willing to hold on to God's promises even when it gets hard and it doesn't look like what He said. You have to be willing to let God show you and then allow Him to help you do the work to make the necessary changes in you. I had to allow God to take me through different seasons in my life and learn the lessons so I didn't have to repeat them.

Week 3: His Example

Not only did God call us to be our husband's help, but also He told us to be his example. The best example you can be to your husband is a godly one. God took me through a season of being isolated to Him. During this time, everything I wanted to say, though I needed to say to my husband, I had to say it to Him first. What I didn't know at that time was that God was developing a gentle and quiet spirit within me, and my husband was taking notice. My husband was doing things that I wanted him to do, without me saying a word, but it was because of my prayers and quietness. God was answering my prayers. Sometimes he would say I don't know why I'm doing this or feeling this way. I would just smile because I knew why. I was being a godly example, and God was changing his ways.

    Ladies, we have to be willing to give God complete control and full access to our lives for Him to make the necessary changes in us to be the example that our husbands need to see. When we allow the Lord to do the work to change us, our husbands will see and prayerfully follow suit. There have been times in my marriage when my example was just being obedient to the voice of the Lord. This sometimes caused anger in my husband. But the Lord had to show me that my husband was not mad at me. He was angry with himself because he saw God in me, and he was convicted of his own sins. So when you encounter this behavior, don't lose heart; just continue to pray and ask God to lead you. Remember the devil wants you to give up, but God wants you to keep fighting for your marriage.

BASIC PREP

Notes:_____
_____
_____
_____
_____
_____
_____
_____
_____
_____
_____
_____
_____
_____

Read 1 Peter 3:1–12.

As you read this, ask God to help you understand what it is that He wants you to know. And ask God to help you not get discouraged if your husband shows anger at your example; just know that he's not mad at you, but the devil is. Remember this is a spiritual battle, so your enemy is not the person you're looking at in front of you; it's the Spirit behind.

_____
_____
_____
_____
_____
_____
_____
_____

Pray.

Cover your example of having a quiet and gentle spirit in prayer.

Your example of a quiet and gentle spirit is not to make your husband feel bad. This is to allow God to teach you how to talk to Him first. Ask God to show you how to communicate and pray for your husband.

BASIC PREP

Homework

The third thing you have to ask is am I ready to be open and honest with God?

_____
_____
_____
_____
_____
_____
_____
_____
_____
_____
_____
_____
_____
_____
_____
_____
_____
_____
_____
_____

When you ask the question, you have to be ready and willing to hear GOD's response. You have to be honest with God about everything; even though He knows everything, he wants to hear it from you. You have to pour your heart out, and don't be afraid to tell Him that you feel like it's all His fault. Remember He already knows this is how you feel. He just wants you to say it out loud to Him so He can help you. Make your request known to the LORD, and then wait to hear what He has to say to you. Then do it. It is time to be naked and unashamed with God.

Week 4: His Strength

You might ask yourself, "How does submitting to my husband give him strength?" The thing is when you submit to your husband, as to the Lord, you actually empower your husband with the strength he needs to be who God has called him to be. But not only does your husband gain strength, but also you will gain strength and confidence in God to lead your husband. And in your submission, pray that the Lord speaks to your husband and that he will hear the voice of the Lord and obey. Now is the time you get to do the job that God hired you for; be the help to lighten his load; don't add to it.

Ladies, don't be afraid to let God do what He do. Submit everything to Him, and let Him work. I promise He knows what He's doing; it will get scary, but trust Him. He got you, and He will never leave you alone. He is always there even when it doesn't feel like it.

Notes:_____
_____
_____
_____
_____
_____
_____
_____
_____
_____
_____
_____
_____

BASIC PREP

_____
_____
_____
_____
_____
_____
_____
_____

Read Ephesians 5:22–33.

As you read this, ask God to help you understand what it is that He wants you to know. Teach me how to submit to You first so I can learn how to submit to my husband.

_____
_____
_____
_____
_____
_____
_____
_____
_____
_____
_____
_____
_____
_____
_____
_____
_____

Pray.

Ask your husband if he has something he wants or needs you to pray for. Let him know that if he can't think of anything at the moment to tell you later or he can't write it down, leave it for you to find it later or text it to you. And always pray that he will seek and listen to the Lord's voice and that he will include you in all decisions.

Homework

Will you let go and let God help you?

_____
_____
_____
_____
_____
_____
_____
_____
_____
_____
_____
_____

    God cannot help you if you don't invite Him in to help. You have to trust GOD with all your heart and let Him lead you. For me, it was Joshua Tree Road in California going to my mother-in-law's house for the first time. This was a long dark winding road that would get me to where I needed to go, but I had to make the decision to go down it.

    When I got to the opening of this road, I was scared, it was dark, and I could not see anything except the yellow line that separated the two lanes. So before heading down, I pulled over and called my mother-in-law and told her where I was, and she said just keep coming; you're on the right path. Needless to say, after praying and a few phone calls to work up the courage, I headed down Joshua Tree Road. It took a few hours, but I made it to her house. The next day, she drove me down that same road that I had been terrified of the night before because I could not see anything in the darkness except the yellow line that was leading me to where I needed to go. To my surprise, there were houses everywhere, but God allowed me to see what I needed to see to get me where I needed to be.

Week 5: His Love

The Lord just showed me that if your husband is not fully grounded and rooted in God's love, you have to be careful with his love. This kind of love can be coming from many different sources, such as childhood hurt or disappointment. This love can also come from old relationships, breakups, bad decisions, and sometimes just a life of not knowing God's true love because we know that God's love is unconditional. So in other words, you have to know and understand the driving force behind your husband's expression of love.

Ladies, you have to understand God's unconditional love for you first.

God's love is not dependent upon if you will love Him back or if you are in a good mood. It doesn't even matter if you feel like it or not; God loves us anyway. I remember my husband telling me that he loved me the best he knew how, and I completely understood because he was loving me with his own limited ability and not how I love him with God's unconditional love.

Notes:_____
_____
_____
_____
_____
_____
_____
_____
_____
_____
_____

BASIC PREP

Read 1 Corinthians 13:4–8a.

As you read this, ask God to help you understand what it is that He wants you to know? Show me how to extend the same love and grace that You showed me to myhusband.

_____
_____
_____
_____
_____
_____
_____
_____
_____
_____

Pray.

Ask God to help you to choose to love your husband with nothing in return and allow God to give you His peace that surpasses all understanding and to guard your mind and heart and to give you joy in doing so.

_____
_____
_____
_____
_____
_____
_____
_____
_____
_____

Homework

Are you willing to love your husband unconditionally as God loves you?

_____
_____
_____
_____
_____
_____
_____
_____
_____
_____
_____
_____
_____
_____

    Not too long ago, I was sitting in my car, and I asked God, "Why is this the most complicated relationship?" Referring to my marriage. This is supposed to be the one that brings the most joy, but instead, it brings the most heartache. The Lord, in all His kindness, began to talk to me, and He showed me everything that my husband did to me. I did it to Him first. The Lord said I was your first husband, and you cheated on Me with your husband because you were having sex before you were married. You were an unfaithful wife. The same tears you cry, I cried them for you; the same hurt that you feel, I felt it for you, so I do understand everything. So if I can forgive you, who are you to say that you can't forgive your husband? With the same unconditional love and forgiveness I have for you, you have to have the same for your husband.

Week 6: His Fruit

We know that the fruit of the Spirit is love, joy, peace, patience, kindness, goodness, faithfulness, gentleness, and self-control, but how often do we let this fruit be our response to our husbands?

Ladies, we have to get a new attitude toward our husbands. You have to have an attitude of unconditional love and the fruit of the Spirit. This is what your husband needs to see all day, every day from you.

Notes:

Read 1 Galatians 5:22.

As you read this, ask God to help you understand what it is that He wants you to know. Ask God to show you how to express the fruit of the Spirit to your husband at all times.

Pray.

Ask God to show you and your husband how to become best friends. Let your husband be the one you go to first after God. And let your husband be the holder of all your secrets. Pray to learn how to communicate with your husband.

Homework

Are you ready to let the fruit of the Spirit be your response to your husband all the time, every time?

_____
_____
_____
_____
_____
_____
_____
_____
_____
_____
_____
_____
_____
_____

As I sit here to type this last part, I became overwhelmed with joy and tears because the LORD just showed me once again that He did answer my prayer. My prayer for years was that my husband would see God in me and the fruit of the Spirit. My husband feels and knows my unconditional love for him. He saw the joy when I should have been sad. He saw peace when there was no peace. He saw patience when he had non with me. He saw kindness when his words and actions weren't kind to me. He saw goodness when he wasn't good to me. He saw faithfulness when he wasn't faithful to me. He saw gentleness and strength in my heart when he tried to tear me down. He saw self-control when the Lord gave me a gentle and quiet spirit toward him when he had rage toward me.

My story is not over. It just begun. The Lord said that my latter would be greater than my beginning, so the best is yet to come.

About the Author

Helen was born in Los Angles, California, to Linzsay and Sylvia Richardson. They had seven children, four boys and three girls. Helen is the youngest girl and number six of the seven children. Helen is a very passionate person and always has been. Her mother, Sylvia, started attending church when Helen was about three years old, so she grew up going to church most of her life. Although she did walk away from God for a brief period, He never left her. Helen got married later in life and has a teenage son whom she loves and adores.

She recently worked with a deafblind student and has worked with special-needs kids for over eleven years and continues to do so. Helen also helps raise her niece with cerebral palsy, who is in a wheelchair. Helen loves to travel. She loves music, dancing, walking and has a newfound love for pilates. Helen will occasionally watch anime and with her son, but their biggest pastime is watching all the Marvel movies together. She loves her family, but most of all, she loves God and is a great friend to have on your side because she will hold you down when it really counts and will be there for you when you need it most. And God has given her a heart for His daughters to help them find their way back to the Father, back to the basics.